21.50

D0776876

SandCastle

Keeping the Peace

Acting with Kindness

Pam Scheunemann

Consulting Editor, Diane Craig, M.A./Reading Specialist

ABDO
Publishing Company

303 Boul. Beacon̶s̶f̶i̶e̶l̶d̶, Beaconsfield, PQ
H9W 4A7

Published by ABDO Publishing Company, 4940 Viking Drive, Edina, Minnesota 55435.

Printed in the United States.

Credits
Edited by: Pam Price
Curriculum Coordinator: Nancy Tuminelly
Cover and Interior Design and Production: Mighty Media
Photo Credits: BananaStock Ltd., Corbis Images, Comstock, Image Source, PhotoDisc, Stockbyte

Library of Congress Cataloging-in-Publication Data

Scheunemann, Pam, 1955-
       Acting with kindness / Pam Scheunemann.
          p. cm. -- (Keeping the peace)
       Includes index.
       Summary: Describes some everyday actions that demontrate kindness.
       ISBN 1-59197-557-3
       1. Kindness--Juvenile literature. 2. Conduct of life--Juvenile literature. 3. Peace--Juvenile literature. [1. Kindness. 2. Conduct of life. 3. Peace.] I. Title.

BJ1533.K5S34 2004
177'.7--dc22

                                                                                2003057784

SandCastle™ books are created by a professional team of educators, reading specialists, and content developers around five essential components that include phonemic awareness, phonics, vocabulary, text comprehension, and fluency. All books are written, reviewed, and leveled for guided reading, early intervention reading, and Accelerated Reader® programs and designed for use in shared, guided, and independent reading and writing activities to support a balanced approach to literacy instruction.

Let Us Know

After reading the book, SandCastle would like you to tell us your stories about reading. What is your favorite page? Was there something hard that you needed help with? Share the ups and downs of learning to read. We want to hear from you! To get posted on the ABDO Publishing Company Web site, send us e-mail at:

sandcastle@abdopub.com

SandCastle Level: Transitional

Being
considerate of
others keeps the
peace.

A peacekeeper is kind to others.

Alice gives her mom a flower.

Alice's dad is cleaning the house.

Alice is kind and offers to help.

Alex wants to do something kind for his mother.

He brings her a special breakfast.

Tina has a new bike.

It is kind of her to let her sister ride it.

Rick is new at school.

It is kind of Terry to show him around.

Julie's aunt has a birthday.

Julie is kind and brings her flowers.

Sara is afraid of the hospital.

The doctor speaks to her kindly to calm her fears.

Ann is feeling sad.

Carol is kind and talks with Ann so she will feel better.

After receiving a gift, Dan writes a thank you note.

A simple act of kindness can make others happy.

What can you do
to keep the peace?

Glossary

breakfast. the first meal of the day

kind. friendly, helpful, and considerate

note. a short, informal letter

peacekeeper. someone who keeps the peace

special. unusual or unique

About SandCastle™

A professional team of educators, reading specialists, and content developers created the SandCastle™ series to support young readers as they develop reading skills and strategies and increase their general knowledge. The SandCastle™ series has four levels that correspond to early literacy development in young children. The levels are provided to help teachers and parents select the appropriate books for young readers.

Emerging Readers
(no flags)

Beginning Readers
(1 flag)

Transitional Readers
(2 flags)

Fluent Readers
(3 flags)

These levels are meant only as a guide. All levels are subject to change.

ABDO
Publishing Company

To see a complete list of SandCastle™ books and other nonfiction titles from ABDO Publishing Company, visit **www.abdopub.com** or contact us at:

4940 Viking Drive, Edina, Minnesota 55435 • 1-800-800-1312 • fax: 1-952-831-1632